all recipes™

Cookie Lover's cookbook

Published by Oxmoor House, Inc.
ISBN: 0-8487-2334-1
Printed in the United States of America
Third Printing 2003

Cookie Basics

Just about everyone loves cookies. And it seems like just about everyone has a different opinion on how cookies should be. Some people like their cookies crisp and delicate. Others prefer a thick, chewy cookie that you can sink your teeth into. The conundrum lies in getting the cookies you bake to have the texture you want.

Mixing Technique

Cookies are not as delicate as cakes, but mixing still plays an important role. The most important step in cookie mixing is the creaming step. This is the step where the fat and the sugar are whipped together until light colored, smooth, and fluffy. This helps to incorporate air into the batter that's needed for the baking soda and/or baking powder to work. Do not overmix the dough or you will have tough, rubbery cookies. Once you combine the dry and wet ingredients, mix until just blended.

Equipment

Different baking sheets and whether or not you grease them produces different results. A good baking sheet can make a big difference. Super thin baking sheets will cause the cookie bottoms to cook faster, sometimes resulting in burnt bottoms. Insulated baking sheets allow air movement and help produce puffier cookies. If you want flat crisp cookies, your best bet is the standard semi-thick baking sheets that are available just about everywhere. If you grease your cookie sheets before baking, it will cause the cookies to spread more, but if you don't grease the sheets, you run the risk of the cookies sticking to the sheets and making a big mess. A good and fairly inexpensive solution to this is parchment paper. Its non-stick surface makes for easy cookie removal and yet it doesn't cause the cookies to spread.

Temperature

Do not underestimate the importance of temperature in cookie baking. Cookie dough that's chilled before baking will hold its shape and produce a slightly puffier cookie. Cookie dough that's at room temperature before baking will spread and flatten out while baking. So if you happen to have a very warm kitchen, it's a good idea to refrigerate the dough before you bake it.

Baking Time

Since cookies are small, they tend to bake fast. A difference in temperature can completely change the amount of time you'll need to bake your cookies. If you want cookies to be chewy, the trick is to slightly underbake them. If you want them to be crispy, bake them a little longer. The best way to do this is with an accurate oven thermometer, a timer, and your watchful eye until you get it all down.
- Ursula Dalzell

For more information, visit **Allrecipes.com**

Award-Winning
Soft Chocolate Chip Cookies

Submitted by: **Debbi Borsick**

"My daughter, Tegan, made these for a cookie baking contest and won a red ribbon! You can use any flavor pudding you like for this recipe."

Prep Time: 15 minutes • **Cook Time:** 12 minutes per batch

4½ cups all-purpose flour
2 teaspoons baking soda
2 cups butter, softened
1½ cups packed brown sugar
½ cup white sugar
2 (3.4 ounce) packages instant vanilla pudding mix

4 eggs
2 teaspoons vanilla extract
4 cups semisweet chocolate chips
2 cups chopped walnuts (optional)

1. Preheat oven to 350°F (175°C). Stir together the flour and baking soda and set aside.

2. In a large bowl, cream together the butter, brown sugar, and white sugar. Beat in the instant pudding mix until blended. Stir in the eggs and vanilla. Blend in the flour mixture. Finally, stir in the chocolate chips and nuts, if desired. Drop cookies by rounded teaspoonfuls onto ungreased baking sheets.

3. Bake in the preheated oven for 10 to 12 minutes until edges are golden brown. Allow cookies to cool for 5 minutes on baking sheets before transferring to wire racks to cool completely. **Yield:** 6 dozen.

Per cookie: About 177 calories, 2g protein, 21g carbohydrate, 11g fat, 1g fiber, 26mg cholesterol, 132mg sodium

drop dead delicious

Nothing could be easier than whipping up a batch of drop cookies that require no cutting, shaping, or rolling. Drop cookies are slightly irregular in shape, but you can keep your cookies the same size by scooping equal amounts of dough for each cookie. Use either a tablespoon or teaspoon to pick up the dough and use another spoon to push the dough onto the baking sheets. Place dough on the baking sheets 1 to 2 inches apart so cookies won't run together when they bake.

Absolutely Sinful Chocolate, Chocolate Chip Cookies

Submitted by: **Marsha**

"This recipe was given to me by my grandmother 10 years ago. The cookies are always a huge hit at work and with my family! A wonderful soft cookie that is incredibly chocolaty."

Prep Time: 15 minutes • **Cook Time:** 10 minutes per batch

2½	(1 ounce) squares unsweetened chocolate, chopped	¼	teaspoon salt
		1¼	cups white sugar
½	cup butter	2	eggs
2	cups all-purpose flour	1	teaspoon vanilla extract
½	teaspoon baking soda	⅔	cup sour cream
1	teaspoon baking powder	2	cups semisweet chocolate chips

1. Preheat oven to 375°F (190°C). Lightly grease baking sheets. In the microwave or over a double boiler, melt unsweetened chocolate and butter together, stirring occasionally until smooth. Sift together flour, baking soda, baking powder, and salt; set aside.

2. In a medium bowl, beat sugar, eggs, and vanilla until light. Mix in the chocolate mixture until well blended. Stir in the sifted ingredients alternately with sour cream, then mix in chocolate chips. Drop by rounded tablespoonfuls onto prepared baking sheets.

3. Bake in the preheated oven for 8 to 10 minutes. Allow cookies to cool on baking sheets for 5 minutes before transferring to wire racks to cool completely. **Yield:** 3 dozen.

Per cookie: About 143 calories, 2g protein, 19g carbohydrate, 8g fat, 1g fiber, 21mg cholesterol, 74mg sodium

Beth's Spicy Oatmeal-Raisin Cookies

Submitted by: **Beth Sigworth**

"With a little experimenting, I came up with these chewy, spicy, oatmeal raisin cookies. They make your kitchen smell wonderful while they're baking. They remind me of Christmas because the spices smell so good."

Prep Time: 15 minutes • **Cook Time:** 12 minutes per batch

½ cup butter, softened
½ cup butter-flavored shortening
1 cup packed light brown sugar
½ cup white sugar
2 eggs
1 teaspoon vanilla extract

1½ cups all-purpose flour
1 teaspoon baking soda
1 teaspoon ground cinnamon
½ teaspoon ground cloves
½ teaspoon salt
3 cups rolled oats
1 cup raisins

1. Preheat oven to 350°F (175°C).

2. In a large bowl, cream together the butter, butter-flavored shortening, brown sugar, white sugar, eggs, and vanilla until smooth. Combine the flour, baking soda, cinnamon, cloves, and salt; stir into the sugar mixture. Stir in the oats and raisins. Drop by rounded teaspoonfuls onto ungreased baking sheets.

3. Bake in the preheated oven for 10 to 12 minutes until light and golden. Do not overbake. Allow cookies to cool for 2 minutes on baking sheets before transferring to wire racks to cool completely.
Yield: 3 dozen.

Per cookie: About 170 calories, 3g protein, 25g carbohydrate, 7g fat, 2g fiber, 19mg cholesterol, 100mg sodium

White Chocolate and Cranberry Cookies

Submitted by: **Diane Abed**

"I make a basic chocolate chip cookie dough, but use white chocolate chips, dried cranberries, and brandy (instead of vanilla). Great for Christmas time!"

Prep Time: 15 minutes • **Cook Time:** 10 minutes per batch

½ cup butter, softened	1½ cups all-purpose flour
½ cup packed brown sugar	½ teaspoon baking soda
½ cup white sugar	¾ cup white chocolate chips
1 egg	1 cup dried cranberries
1 tablespoon brandy	

1. Preheat oven to 375°F (190°C). Grease baking sheets.

2. In a large bowl, cream together the butter, brown sugar, and white sugar until smooth. Beat in the egg and brandy. Combine the flour and baking soda; stir into the sugar mixture. Mix in the white chocolate chips and cranberries. Drop by heaping tablespoonfuls onto prepared baking sheets.

3. Bake in the preheated oven for 8 to 10 minutes. Allow cookies to cool for 1 minute on the baking sheets before transferring to wire racks to cool completely. **Yield:** 2 dozen.

Per cookie: About 146 calories, 1g protein, 22g carbohydrate, 6g fat, 1g fiber, 20mg cholesterol, 75mg sodium

*P*archment pointers

Greasing your baking sheets will cause cookies to spread, resulting in thinner, crispier cookies. But if you don't grease the sheets you run the risk of the cookies sticking and ruining the batch. A good solution to this is parchment paper. This heavy paper is moisture- and heat-resistant and comes on a roll like wax paper. Just tear off a strip of parchment paper and place it on the baking sheets—your baked cookies will lift off with ease. Also, you can reuse the sheet several times when you are making multiple batches of cookies, and cleanup is a breeze. - Ursula Dalzell, **Allrecipes.com**

Chocolate-Peanut Butter Cup Cookies

Submitted by: **Joanna Knudsen**

"These are the best cookies I have ever eaten. If you like peanut butter and chocolate, these cookies are for you!"

Prep Time: 15 minutes • **Cook Time:** 14 minutes per batch

1 cup butter, softened	1 teaspoon baking soda
¾ cup creamy peanut butter	1 cup semisweet chocolate chips
¾ cup white sugar	1 cup peanut butter chips
¾ cup packed brown sugar	1 (6 ounce) package chocolate covered peanut butter cups, cut into eighths
2 eggs	
1 teaspoon vanilla extract	
2⅓ cups all-purpose flour	
⅓ cup cocoa powder	

1. Preheat oven to 350°F (175°C).

2. In a large bowl, cream together the butter, peanut butter, white sugar, and brown sugar until smooth. Beat in the eggs, one at a time, then stir in the vanilla. Combine the flour, cocoa, and baking soda; stir into the peanut butter mixture. Mix in the chocolate chips, peanut butter chips, and peanut butter cups. Drop by tablespoonfuls onto ungreased baking sheets.

3. Bake in the preheated oven for 13 to 14 minutes. Let cool for 5 minutes on baking sheets before transferring to wire racks to cool completely. **Yield:** 3 dozen.

Per cookie: About 231 calories, 5g protein, 25g carbohydrate, 13g fat, 2g fiber, 26mg cholesterol, 149mg sodium

Aunt Cora's World's Greatest Cookies

Submitted by: **Mary Hays**

"Aunt Cora's recipe makes the world's best chocolate chip-peanut butter cookies!"

Prep Time: 15 minutes • **Cook Time:** 15 minutes per batch

1 cup butter or margarine, softened
1 cup peanut butter
1 cup white sugar
1 cup packed brown sugar
2 eggs
2 cups unbleached all-purpose flour
1 teaspoon baking soda
2 cups semisweet chocolate chips

1. Preheat oven to 325°F (165°C).

2. In a large bowl, cream together the butter, peanut butter, white sugar, and brown sugar until smooth. Beat in the eggs, one at a time, mixing well after each. Combine the flour and baking soda; stir into the peanut butter mixture. Mix in chocolate chips. Drop by heaping teaspoonfuls onto ungreased baking sheets.

3. Bake in the preheated oven for 12 to 15 minutes or until lightly browned at the edges. Allow cookies to cool on the baking sheets for 1 minute before transferring to wire racks to cool completely. **Yield:** 4 dozen.

Per cookie: About 154 calories, 3g protein, 18g carbohydrate, 9g fat, 1g fiber, 9mg cholesterol, 100mg sodium

Cowboy Cookies III

Submitted by: **Bonnie Smith**

"If you cook these just right, they're soft and the tiniest bit chewy, and they melt in your mouth!"

Prep Time: 15 minutes • **Cook Time:** 10 minutes per batch

2 cups all-purpose flour	1 cup packed brown sugar
1 teaspoon baking powder	2 eggs
1 teaspoon baking soda	1 teaspoon vanilla extract
½ teaspoon salt	2 cups rolled oats
1 cup butter, softened	1 cup semisweet chocolate
1 cup white sugar	chips

1. Preheat oven to 350°F (175°C). Grease baking sheets. Sift together the flour, baking powder, baking soda, and salt. Set aside.

2. In a large bowl, cream together the butter, white sugar, and brown sugar until light and fluffy. Beat in the eggs, one at a time, then stir in the vanilla. Gradually stir in the sifted ingredients. Stir in the rolled oats and chocolate chips. Drop by rounded teaspoonfuls onto the prepared baking sheets.

3. Bake in the preheated oven for 8 to 10 minutes. Allow cookies to cool on baking sheets for 5 minutes before transferring to wire racks to cool completely. **Yield:** 5 dozen.

Per cookie: About 105 calories, 2g protein, 15g carbohydrate, 5g fat, 1g fiber, 15mg cholesterol, 84mg sodium

Farm Macaroons

Submitted by: **Juanita**

"This is a recipe that we made on the farm in the 1930s. It's a delicious coconut macaroon."

Prep Time: 20 minutes • **Cook Time:** 20 minutes per batch

4	egg whites	1¼	cups white sugar
½	teaspoon vanilla extract	¼	cup all-purpose flour
¼	teaspoon almond extract	¼	teaspoon salt
⅛	teaspoon cream of tartar	2½	cups flaked coconut

1. Preheat oven to 300°F (150°C). Grease and flour baking sheets.
2. In a medium bowl, beat egg whites, vanilla, almond extract, and cream of tartar until soft peaks form. Gradually beat in sugar, and whip until stiff. Toss together flour, salt, and coconut in a separate bowl; fold into egg whites. Drop by heaping tablespoonfuls onto the prepared baking sheets.
3. Bake in the preheated oven for 18 to 20 minutes or until slightly golden. Allow cookies to cool on the baking sheets for easy removal.
Yield: 4 dozen.

Per cookie: About 42 calories, 1g protein, 8g carbohydrate, 1g fat, 0g fiber, 0mg cholesterol, 27mg sodium

Mailing cookies

Everyone loves to receive packages in the mail, especially the edible variety. Make sure you get cheers, not jeers, when you mail your elegant eatables.

Perfect for Shipping
• Cookies that have a crunchy or hard texture such as biscotti, crisps, and shortbreads make excellent choices for mail delivery. They tend to be fairly sturdy, so you don't have to worry too much about breakage.
• Cookies that have a slightly chewy texture, such as chocolate chip or oatmeal-raisin cookies, also ship well. They tend to dry out if they're in the mail for more than a week. So if their destination is a long way off, ship them by express to ensure that they arrive just as tasty as when they left. To ensure the freshest cookies, pack them frozen and ship via overnight mail.
• Macaroons and pignoli mail beautifully. Their chewy, moist textures only seem to improve after they've aged a few days. Who wouldn't want to receive a single, perfect chocolate-dipped coconut macaroon as a special treat? - Ursula Dalzell, **Allrecipes.com**

Angel Whispers

Submitted by: **Julie**

"These are lemony little sandwich cookies that just melt in your mouth. Have a few with a tall glass of iced tea."

Prep Time: 10 minutes • **Cook Time:** 8 minutes per batch

1	cup butter, softened	1	egg, beaten
½	cup confectioners' sugar	⅔	cup white sugar
2	cups all-purpose flour	1½	teaspoons lemon zest
1	teaspoon lemon zest	3	tablespoons lemon juice
½	teaspoon salt	1½	tablespoons butter

1. In a medium bowl, cream together butter and confectioners' sugar until light. Stir in the flour, lemon zest, and salt. Cover bowl and chill for about 1 hour.

2. Preheat oven to 400°F (200°C).

3. Flatten teaspoons of dough onto ungreased baking sheets and bake for 5 to 8 minutes until light brown. Remove from baking sheets to cool on racks.

4. To make the filling: Combine the beaten egg, white sugar, 1½ teaspoons lemon zest, lemon juice, and 1½ tablespoons butter in the top of a double boiler. Stir until thick. Sandwich cookies with 1 teaspoon of filling. **Yield:** 2 dozen.

Per cookie: About 147 calories, 1g protein, 16g carbohydrate, 9g fat, 0g fiber, 32mg cholesterol, 137mg sodium

Whipped Shortbread Cookies

Submitted by: **William Anatooskin**
"A melt-in-your-mouth cookie that's very easy to make."

Prep Time: 15 minutes • **Cook Time:** 17 minutes per batch

1 cup butter, softened
1½ cups all-purpose flour
½ cup confectioners' sugar
¼ cup red maraschino
  cherries, drained and
  quartered

¼ cup green maraschino
  cherries, drained and
  quartered

1. Preheat oven to 350°F (175°C).
2. Blend together the butter, flour, and confectioners' sugar until smooth. Drop by tablespoonfuls 2 inches apart onto ungreased baking sheets.
3. Place 1 red and 1 green cherry quarter on each cookie and bake in the preheated oven for 15 to 17 minutes. Allow cookies to cool for 5 minutes on baking sheets before transferring to wire racks to cool completely. **Yield:** 3 dozen.

Per cookie: About 75 calories, 1g protein, 7g carbohydrate, 5g fat, 0g fiber, 14mg cholesterol, 53mg sodium

Melt-In-Your-Mouth Shortbread

Submitted by: **Jennifer Wilton**
"This quick and easy shortbread will literally melt when you take a bite. Take some time to decorate them, and they're perfect for a Christmas party."

Prep Time: 10 minutes • **Cook Time:** 15 minutes per batch

1 cup butter, softened
½ cup confectioners' sugar

¼ cup cornstarch
1½ cups all-purpose flour

1. Preheat oven to 375°F (190°C).
2. Whip butter with an electric mixer until fluffy. Stir in the confectioners' sugar, cornstarch, and flour. Beat on low speed for 1 minute,

then on high for 3 to 4 minutes. Drop cookies by tablespoonfuls 2 inches apart onto ungreased baking sheets.

3. Bake in the preheated oven for 12 to 15 minutes. Watch that the edges don't brown too much. Cool on wire racks. **Yield:** 2 dozen.

Per cookie: About 111 calories, 1g protein, 10g carbohydrate, 8g fat, 0g fiber, 21mg cholesterol, 78mg sodium

Passover Chocolate Chip Meringues

Submitted by: **Leah Perez**
"Light chocolate bites of crisp meringue are easy to make and easy to eat."

Prep Time: 15 minutes • **Cook Time:** 3 hours

2 egg whites	½ teaspoon salt
¾ cup white sugar	1 cup mini semisweet
1 teaspoon vanilla extract	chocolate chips

1. Preheat oven to 350°F (175°C). Line 2 baking sheets with parchment paper or aluminum foil.

2. With an electric mixer, beat egg whites until soft peaks form. Add sugar into the egg whites 1 teaspoon at a time. Gently stir in vanilla and salt; beat until the egg whites are stiff and shiny. Fold in chocolate chips.

3. Drop mixture by teaspoonfuls onto the prepared baking sheets. Turn off the oven, place the cookies inside the oven, and leave them for a few hours or overnight. **Yield:** 2 dozen.

Per cookie: About 68 calories, 0g protein, 12mg carbohydrate, 2g fat, 0g fiber, 0mg cholesterol, 53mg sodium

Peanut Butter Chews

Submitted by: **Cindy**

"I make these no-bake cookies for my kids all the time, and I sometimes drizzle chocolate and butterscotch on top. Rich, but excellent!"

Prep Time: 25 minutes

1 cup corn syrup	1 cup semisweet chocolate chips (optional)
1 cup white sugar	1 cup butterscotch chips (optional)
1 cup creamy peanut butter	
4½ cups cornflakes cereal	

1. In a large saucepan over medium heat, combine corn syrup and white sugar. Bring to a boil, boil for 1 minute, and remove from heat. Stir in peanut butter until well blended. Mix in cereal until evenly coated. Drop by spoonfuls onto wax paper.

2. In a glass bowl in the microwave, or using a double boiler, melt chocolate chips and butterscotch chips, stirring frequently until smooth. Drizzle on the top of the cookies, if desired. **Yield:** 3 dozen.

Per cookie: About 152 calories, 2g protein, 23g carbohydrate, 6g fat, 1g fiber, 0mg cholesterol, 39mg sodium

The Best Rolled Sugar Cookies

Submitted by: **Jill Saunders**
"I make icing for these cookies with confectioners' sugar and milk. I make it fairly thin and paint the icing on the cookies with a pastry brush."

Prep Time: 20 minutes • **Cook Time:** 8 minutes per batch

1½ cups butter, softened
2 cups white sugar
4 eggs
1 teaspoon vanilla extract

5 cups all–purpose flour
2 teaspoons baking powder
1 teaspoon salt

1. In a large bowl, cream together butter and sugar until smooth. Beat in eggs and vanilla. Stir in the flour, baking powder, and salt. Cover and chill dough for at least 1 hour or overnight.
2. Preheat oven to 400°F (200°C). Roll out dough on floured surface ¼ to ½ inch thick. Cut into shapes with any cookie cutter. Place cookies 1 inch apart on ungreased baking sheets.
3. Bake in preheated oven for 6 to 8 minutes. Allow cookies to cool for 5 minutes on baking sheets before transferring to wire racks to cool completely. **Yield:** 5 dozen.

Per cookie: About 110 calories, 2g protein, 15g carbohydrate, 5g fat, 0g fiber, 27mg cholesterol, 106mg sodium

Cookie cutouts

Baking cutout cookies is a popular activity during the holidays and throughout the year. Get your kids involved, and have them be your jolly little helpers. Here are some helpful hints to make it easier.
• Chill the dough before rolling it out. Divide the dough into halves or thirds for faster chilling. To save time, chill in the freezer for 20 minutes. If you like to plan ahead, freeze the dough up to 3 weeks.
• Roll out dough to the suggested thickness in the recipe you are using. Using a ruler to measure the thickness ensures that all the dough is the same for consistent baking times. Roll it out on a lightly floured surface or between pieces of parchment paper.
• Cut dough with cookie cutters dipped in flour to avoid sticking. Make cutouts as close together as possible. Re-roll scraps left from the cutouts to cut more cookies. Re-rolling can result in tough cookie dough; however, re-rolling on a surface dusted with equal parts flour and confectioners' sugar can keep that from happening.
• Use a metal spatula to transfer the dough onto baking sheets and bake until lightly browned around the edges. - *Lisa Marie Gregory,* **Allrecipes.com**

Gingerbread Men

Submitted by: **Kim**

"The secret ingredient in these gingerbread men—pudding mix—makes moist cookies every time."

Prep Time: 15 minutes • **Cook Time:** 12 minutes per batch

1	(3.4 ounce) package cook and serve butterscotch pudding mix	1	egg
½	cup butter, softened	1½	cups all-purpose flour
½	cup packed brown sugar	½	teaspoon baking soda
		1½	teaspoons ground ginger
		1	teaspoon ground cinnamon

1. Cream pudding mix, butter, and brown sugar. Add egg and blend well. In a separate bowl, combine flour, soda, ginger, and cinnamon; blend with pudding mixture. Chill dough until firm or freeze until ready to use.

2. Preheat oven to 350°F (175°C). Grease baking sheets. Roll chilled dough on floured surface to about ⅛ inch thickness and cut with cookie cutter. Place on prepared baking sheets.

3. Bake in the preheated oven for 10 to 12 minutes. Remove from baking sheets to cool on wire racks. Decorate as desired. **Yield:** 2½ dozen.

Per cookie: About 78 calories, 1g protein, 12g carbohydrate, 3g fat, 0g fiber, 15mg cholesterol, 72mg sodium

Vel's Christmas Shortbread

Submitted by: **Judy Smith**

"Vel is my mom, and these are the best shortbread cookies around!"

Prep Time: 30 minutes • **Cook Time:** 12 minutes per batch

2	cups butter, softened	5	cups sifted all-purpose flour
1	cup packed brown sugar		

1. Preheat oven to 350°F (175°C).

2. In a large bowl, cream butter and brown sugar until smooth. Stir in flour and knead by hand until dough comes together. Roll out the dough to ¼ inch thickness and cut with cookie cutters or press dough into shortbread molds. Place cookies 2 inches apart onto ungreased baking sheets.

3. Bake in the preheated oven for 8 to 12 minutes, depending on the size of your cookies. Do not let them brown. Remove from baking sheets to cool on wire racks. **Yield:** 5 dozen.

Per cookie: About 106 calories, 1g protein, 12g carbohydrate, 6g fat, 0g fiber, 17mg cholesterol, 64mg sodium

Granny's Shortbread Cookies

Submitted by: **Lori G**
"Cut these buttery shortbread cookies into Christmas shapes and decorate with colored sugar and maraschino cherries."

Prep Time: 15 minutes • **Cook Time:** 10 minutes per batch

1	cup butter, softened	2	cups all-purpose flour
½	cup confectioners' sugar	1	(2.25 ounce) jar red
½	teaspoon salt		decorator sugar
⅛	teaspoon ground nutmeg	1	(10 ounce) jar maraschino
1	egg yolk		cherries, drained

1. Preheat oven to 350°F (175°C).
2. Cream together the butter, sugar, salt, nutmeg, and egg yolk. Add the flour a little at a time until mixture is stiff.
3. Place onto floured surface and knead lightly until the dough begins to crack. Roll out to ¼ inch thickness and cut into desired shapes.
4. Place on ungreased baking sheets; decorate with colored sugar crystals and maraschino cherries.
5. Bake in the preheated oven for 10 minutes or until golden brown. Remove from baking sheets to cool on wire racks. **Yield:** 2 dozen.

Per cookie: About 143 calories, 1g protein, 17g carbohydrate, 8g fat, 0g fiber, 30mg cholesterol, 135mg sodium

Joe Froggers

Submitted by: **Ingrid**

"This dark molasses, soft cookie is an old time American cookie from New England that's attributed to the legendary Uncle Joe who made cookies as big as lily pads."

Prep Time: 25 minutes • **Cook Time:** 12 minutes per batch

½ cup shortening	1 teaspoon baking soda
1 cup white sugar	1½ teaspoons ground ginger
½ cup water	½ teaspoon ground cloves
1 cup dark molasses	½ teaspoon ground nutmeg
4 cups all-purpose flour	¼ teaspoon ground allspice
1½ teaspoons salt	½ cup white sugar (optional)

1. In a large bowl, cream shortening and sugar together. Mix in water and molasses. Sift together flour, salt, baking soda, ginger, cloves, nutmeg, and allspice; blend into the shortening mixture. Cover and chill 1 hour or overnight.

2. Preheat oven to 375°F (190°C). Lightly grease baking sheets. Roll out cookie dough to ¼ inch thickness on floured surface. Cut with a 3 inch cookie cutter and arrange on prepared baking sheets. Sprinkle cookies with additional sugar, if desired.

3. Bake in the preheated oven for 10 to 12 minutes. Allow cookies to cool for 5 minutes on baking sheets before transferring to wire racks to cool completely. **Yield:** 3 dozen.

Per cookie: About 122 calories, 1g protein, 23g carbohydrate, 3g fat, 0g fiber, 0mg cholesterol, 136mg sodium

Chocolate-Dipped Mocha Rounds

Submitted by: **Laria Tabul**
"Chocolate cookies dipped in chocolate. M-m-m-m-m-m-m!"

Prep Time: 20 minutes • **Cook Time:** 12 minutes per batch

½ cup shortening	1 egg
½ cup butter, softened	2 cups all–purpose flour
½ cup white sugar	1 teaspoon ground cinnamon
½ cup packed brown sugar	¼ teaspoon salt
1 tablespoon instant coffee granules	1½ cups semisweet chocolate chips
1 teaspoon water	3 tablespoons shortening
2 (1 ounce) squares unsweetened chocolate, melted	

1. In a large bowl, beat ½ cup shortening and butter with an electric mixer on medium speed. Add the sugar and brown sugar and beat until fluffy.

2. Dissolve the instant coffee granules in the water. Add the melted chocolate, egg, and coffee to the butter mixture and beat well.

3. Stir flour, cinnamon, and salt together and add to the butter mixture. Cover and chill 1 hour or until easy to handle.

4. Shape into two 7 inch long rolls. Wrap in plastic wrap and chill for at least 6 hours or overnight.

5. Preheat oven to 350°F (175°C).

6. Cut dough into ¼ inch slices and place on ungreased baking sheets. Bake in the preheated oven for 10 to 12 minutes. Remove to a wire rack and cool.

7. Melt the chocolate chips and 3 tablespoons of shortening over low heat. Dip ½ of each cookie into the chocolate mixture. Place on wax paper until the chocolate is set. **Yield:** 5 dozen.

Per cookie: About 90 calories, 1g protein, 10g carbohydrate, 6g fat, 1g fiber, 8mg cholesterol, 28mg sodium

Brown Sugar Cookies II

Submitted by: **Debbie Falen**

"The dough for these cookies can be frozen up to 3 months, and you can make variations with chocolate chips, oatmeal, coconut, peanut butter, nuts, or fruit."

Prep Time: 15 minutes • **Cook Time:** 11 minutes per batch

⅔	cup shortening	2	teaspoons vanilla extract
⅔	cup butter, softened	3¼	cups all-purpose flour
1	cup white sugar	1	teaspoon baking soda
1	cup packed brown sugar	1	teaspoon salt
2	eggs		

1. Mix shortening, butter, white sugar, brown sugar, eggs, and vanilla thoroughly. Stir in flour, baking soda, and salt.

2. Turn dough onto lightly floured surface. Shape dough into a ball with lightly floured hands, pressing to make dough compact. Cut dough in half.

3. Shape each half into a roll 2 inches in diameter and about 8 inches long by gently rolling dough back and forth on floured surface. Roll dough onto plastic wrap: wrap and twist ends tightly. Dough can be refrigerated up to 1 week or frozen up to 3 months.

4. Preheat oven to 375°F (190°C).

5. Cut roll into ¼ inch slices. It's not necessary to thaw frozen dough before slicing. Place slices about 2 inches apart on ungreased baking sheets. Bake in the preheated oven for 9 to 11 minutes. Immediately remove cookies from baking sheets onto wire racks to cool. **Yield:** 5 dozen.

Per cookie: About 93 calories, 1g protein, 12g carbohydrate, 5g fat, 0g fiber, 13mg cholesterol, 85mg sodium

Variations:

Nutty Chocolate Chip Cookies: Add 1 cup mini semisweet chocolate chips and 1 cup chopped nuts with the flour.

Oatmeal-Coconut Cookies: Reduce flour to 2¾ cups. Add 1 cup flaked coconut and 1 cup quick-cooking oats with the flour.

Peanut Butter Cookies: Add 1 cup creamy or chunky peanut butter with the shortening.

Chocolate-Nut Cookies: Add 1 cup chopped nuts and ½ cup cocoa with the flour.

Neapolitan Cookies

Submitted by: **Missy**
"This cute refrigerator cookie resembles the popular ice cream flavor."

Prep Time: 45 minutes • **Cook Time:** 12 minutes per batch

1 cup butter, softened	½ teaspoon almond extract
1½ cups white sugar	5 drops red food coloring
1 egg	1 (1 ounce) square
1 teaspoon vanilla extract	unsweetened chocolate,
2½ cups all-purpose flour	melted
1½ teaspoons baking powder	½ cup chopped walnuts
½ teaspoon salt	

1. In a medium bowl, cream together the butter and sugar. Stir in the egg and vanilla. Combine the flour, baking powder, and salt; stir into the creamed mixture. Divide dough equally into 3 small bowls. Add almond extract and red food coloring to 1 portion; stir until thoroughly mixed. Mix chocolate into second bowl and walnuts into the third bowl.

2. Line a 5x9 inch loaf pan with wax paper and spread the red almond dough evenly in the pan. Spread the white walnut dough evenly over the almond layer, and top with chocolate dough layer. Cover layered dough with wax paper and place in the refrigerator until firm, about 4 hours.

3. Preheat oven to 350°F (175°C). Turn out chilled dough by inverting pan; peel off wax paper. With sharp knife, cut dough lengthwise in half. Slice each half of dough crosswise into ¼ inch slices. Place slices on ungreased baking sheets 1 inch apart.

4. Bake in the preheated oven for 10 to 12 minutes, until light brown. Remove to wire racks to cool. **Yield:** 6 dozen.

Per cookie: About 63 calories, 1g protein, 8g carbohydrate, 3g fat, 0g fiber, 10mg cholesterol, 53mg sodium

Mrs. Sigg's Snickerdoodles

Submitted by: **Beth Sigworth**

"These wonderful cinnamon-sugar cookies became very popular with my friends at church. With crispy edges and chewy centers, these cookies are a crowd-pleaser for sure!"

Prep Time: 20 minutes • **Cook Time:** 10 minutes per batch

½	cup butter, softened	2	teaspoons cream of tartar
½	cup shortening	1	teaspoon baking soda
1½	cups white sugar	¼	teaspoon salt
2	eggs	2	tablespoons white sugar
2	teaspoons vanilla extract	2	teaspoons ground
2¾	cups all-purpose flour		cinnamon

1. Preheat oven to 400°F (200°C).

2. Cream together butter, shortening, 1½ cups sugar, eggs, and vanilla. Blend in the flour, cream of tartar, soda, and salt. Shape dough by rounded teaspoonfuls into balls.

3. Mix together 2 tablespoons sugar and the cinnamon. Roll balls of dough in mixture. Place 2 inches apart on ungreased baking sheets.

4. Bake in the preheated oven for 8 to 10 minutes or until set but not too hard. Remove immediately from baking sheets; cool on wire racks. **Yield:** 5 dozen.

Per cookie: About 74 calories, 1g protein, 10g carbohydrate, 3g fat, 0g fiber, 11mg cholesterol, 49mg sodium

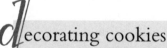

Decorating cookies

If you want great-looking cookies but don't want an all-day production, there are a few ways to add a special touch before baking the cookies. One easy way to spruce up cookies is to roll them in colored sugar, finely chopped nuts, coconut, sesame seeds, or sprinkles before baking. Even a light dusting of confectioners' sugar or cocoa powder will give any cookies an elegant finish. Dust the cookies again, right before serving, to freshen their appearance.   - Emily Brune, **Allrecipes.com**

Big, Soft Ginger Cookies

Submitted by: **Amy Sacha**

"These are just what they say: big, soft gingerbread cookies. They stay soft, too."

Prep Time: 15 minutes • **Cook Time:** 10 minutes per batch

2¼ cups all-purpose flour	1 cup white sugar
2 teaspoons ground ginger	1 egg
1 teaspoon baking soda	1 tablespoon water
¾ teaspoon ground cinnamon	¼ cup molasses
½ teaspoon ground cloves	2 tablespoons white sugar
¼ teaspoon salt	
¾ cup butter or margarine, softened	

1. Preheat oven to 350°F (175°C). Sift together the flour, ginger, baking soda, cinnamon, cloves, and salt. Set aside.

2. In a large bowl, cream together the butter and 1 cup sugar until light and fluffy. Beat in the egg, then stir in the water and molasses. Gradually stir the sifted ingredients into the molasses mixture. Shape dough into walnut sized balls and roll them in the remaining 2 tablespoons of sugar. Place the cookies 2 inches apart onto ungreased baking sheets and flatten slightly.

3. Bake in the preheated oven for 8 to 10 minutes. Allow cookies to cool on baking sheets for 5 minutes before transferring to wire racks to cool completely. **Yield:** 2 dozen.

Per cookie: About 142 calories, 2g protein, 21g carbohydrate, 6g fat, 0g fiber, 9mg cholesterol, 147mg sodium

Chocolate Chip Shortbread Cookie Logs

Submitted by: **Rhonda Golub**

"Delicious shortbread logs with chocolate chips in the cookie and dipped in chocolate and nuts on the end."

Prep Time: 30 minutes • **Cook Time:** 13 minutes per batch

1 cup butter, softened	2 cups mini semisweet
½ cup sifted confectioners'	chocolate chips, divided
sugar	1 tablespoon shortening
1 teaspoon vanilla extract	¾ cup finely chopped walnuts
2 cups all-purpose flour	

1. Cream together butter and confectioners' sugar until smooth. Stir in vanilla. Mix in the flour and 1 cup of the chocolate chips. Chill dough 1 hour.

2. Preheat oven to 350°F (175°C). Grease baking sheets.

3. Shape dough into 2 x ½ inch logs. Place logs 2 inches apart on prepared baking sheets. Bake in preheated oven for 10 to 13 minutes or until firm. Let cookies cool completely before removing from pan.

4. Melt the remaining 1 cup chocolate chips and shortening in a double boiler, stirring frequently until smooth. Dip 1 end of each cookie into the chocolate, then into the nuts. Place onto wax paper until set. **Yield:** 4 dozen.

Per cookie: About 114 calories, 1g protein, 11g carbohydrate, 8g fat, 0g fiber, 10mg cholesterol, 39mg sodium

Four-Spice Crackles

Submitted by: **N. Johnston**

"A heartwarming blend of sugar and spice, these cookies will make your whole house smell delicious."

Prep Time: 15 minutes • **Cook Time:** 12 minutes per batch

2½ cups all-purpose flour
1 teaspoon baking powder
½ teaspoon baking soda
¼ teaspoon salt
1½ teaspoons ground ginger
1 teaspoon ground cloves
1 teaspoon ground nutmeg
¾ teaspoon ground cinnamon

1 cup packed brown sugar
½ cup butter, softened
½ cup shortening
¼ cup molasses
1 egg
⅔ cup coarse granulated sugar
   or white sugar

1. Sift together the flour, baking powder, baking soda, salt, ginger, cloves, nutmeg, and cinnamon. Set aside. In a medium bowl, cream together the brown sugar, butter, and shortening. Stir in the molasses and egg. Gradually stir in the dry ingredients until everything is incorporated. Cover and chill dough for at least 1½ hours.

2. Preheat oven to 350°F (175°C). Lightly grease baking sheets or line with parchment paper.

3. Roll the chilled dough into 1 inch balls. Roll each ball in the coarse sugar. Place 2 inches apart on the prepared baking sheets and flatten slightly.

4. Bake in the preheated oven for 9 to 12 minutes, until cookies are cracked but still soft in the center. Remove from baking sheets to cool on wire racks. Store cooled cookies in an airtight container for up to 2 weeks. **Yield:** 4 dozen.

Per cookie: About 84 calories, 1g protein, 11g carbohydrate, 4g fat, 0g fiber, 10mg cholesterol, 40mg sodium

Apricot-Cream Cheese Thumbprints

Submitted by: **Mellan**

"These always look so pretty on the cookie plates I give for Christmas."

Prep Time: 15 minutes • **Cook Time:** 15 minutes per batch

1½ cups butter, softened
1½ cups white sugar
1 (8 ounce) package cream
cheese, softened
2 eggs
2 tablespoons lemon juice

1½ teaspoons lemon zest
4½ cups all-purpose flour
1½ teaspoons baking powder
1 cup apricot preserves
⅓ cup confectioners' sugar

1. In a large bowl, cream together the butter, sugar, and cream cheese until smooth. Beat in the eggs, one at a time, then stir in the lemon juice and lemon zest. Combine the flour and baking powder; stir into the cream cheese mixture until just combined. Cover and chill until firm, about 1 hour.

2. Preheat oven to 350°F (175°C). Roll tablespoonfuls of dough into balls and place them 2 inches apart on ungreased baking sheets. Using your finger, make an indention in the center of each ball, and fill with ½ teaspoon of apricot preserves.

3. Bake in the preheated oven for 15 minutes or until edges are golden. Allow cookies to cool on the baking sheets for 2 minutes before transferring to wire racks to cool completely. Sprinkle with confectioners' sugar. **Yield:** 7 dozen.

Per cookie: About 90 calories, 1g protein, 12g carbohydrate, 4g fat, 0g fiber, 17mg cholesterol, 53mg sodium

Russian Tea Cakes

Submitted by: **Odette**

"This is a family recipe that's been made at Christmas by at least 4 generations."

Prep Time: 20 minutes • Cook Time: 12 minutes per batch

1 cup butter, softened	2 cups all–purpose flour
1 teaspoon vanilla extract	1 cup chopped walnuts
6 tablespoons confectioners' sugar	⅓ cup confectioners' sugar

1. Preheat oven to 350°F (175°C).
2. In a medium bowl, cream butter and vanilla until smooth. Combine the 6 tablespoons confectioners' sugar and flour; stir into the butter mixture until just blended. Mix in the chopped walnuts. Roll dough into 1 inch balls and place them 2 inches apart on ungreased baking sheets.
3. Bake in the preheated oven for 12 minutes. When cool, roll in remaining confectioners' sugar. **Yield:** 3 dozen.

Per cookie: About 102 calories, 1g protein, 8g carbohydrate, 7g fat, 0g fiber, 14mg cholesterol, 52mg sodium

Cookie exchange party

Do you love setting the table with a huge assortment of cookies but can't stand the thought of spending several days baking? Then a cookie exchange party is the perfect party for you! It makes it possible for everyone who participates to take home a gigantic assortment of homemade cookies without a lot of work.

Invite a group of your favorite cookie-loving friends over and ask them each to bring a big batch of cookies (estimate 1 dozen multiplied by the total number of guests), a stack of recipe cards for the cookies they'll bring, and containers to take cookies home with them. After a period of chatting and snacking, the cookie exchange can commence with all of the cookies organized buffet-style on a table and with everyone gathered around, merrily swapping cookies to take home. Make sure that your guests understand that the cookies they're to bring must be homemade and easily transportable because the cookies will most likely be combined with a lot of other cookies and will need to hold their shape well and transport easily. - *Tammy Weisberger,* **Allrecipes.com**

"Eggnog" Thumbprints

Submitted by: **Susan Hollis**

"Thumbprint cookies with a delicious filling are perfect for Christmas. There's no eggnog in them, but they have an eggnog taste. You can substitute ¼ teaspoon rum extract and 1 tablespoon milk for the rum."

Prep Time: 20 minutes • **Cook Time:** 12 minutes per batch

¾	cup butter, softened	¼	teaspoon salt
½	cup white sugar	¼	cup butter, softened
¼	cup packed brown sugar	1	cup confectioners' sugar
1	egg	1	tablespoon rum
½	teaspoon vanilla extract		Pinch ground nutmeg
2	cups all-purpose flour		

1. Preheat oven to 350°F (175°C).

2. In a medium bowl, cream together ¾ cup butter, white sugar, and brown sugar until smooth. Beat in egg and vanilla. Combine flour and salt; stir into the creamed mixture by hand to form a soft dough. Roll dough into 1 inch balls and place balls 2 inches apart on ungreased baking sheets. Make an indention in the center of each cookie using your finger or thumb.

3. Bake in the preheated oven for 12 minutes. Cool completely.

4. In a small bowl, mix together ¼ cup butter, confectioners' sugar, and rum. Spoon rounded teaspoonfuls of filling onto cookies. Sprinkle with nutmeg. Let stand until set before storing in an airtight container.

Yield: 4 dozen.

Per cookie: About 77 calories, 1g protein, 10g carbohydrate, 4g fat, 0g fiber, 15mg cholesterol, 53mg sodium

Pignoli Cookies

Submitted by: **Adele**

"They are pleasantly sweet, made with almond paste and pine nuts, but no flour."

Prep Time: 30 minutes • Cook Time: 18 minutes per batch

12 ounces almond paste	4 egg whites, divided
½ cup white sugar	1½ cups pine nuts
1 cup confectioners' sugar	

1. Preheat oven to 325°F (165°C). Line 2 baking sheets with foil; lightly grease foil.

2. Mix almond paste and sugar in a food processor until smooth. Add confectioners' sugar and 2 egg whites; process until smooth.

3. Whisk remaining 2 egg whites in a small bowl. Place pine nuts on a shallow plate. With lightly floured hands, roll dough into 1 inch balls. Coat balls in egg whites, shaking off excess, then roll in pine nuts, pressing lightly to stick. Arrange balls on baking sheets and flatten slightly to form a 1½ inch round.

4. Bake in the preheated oven for 15 to 18 minutes or until lightly browned. Allow cookies to cool for 1 minute on baking sheets before transferring to wire racks to cool completely. **Yield:** 3 dozen.

Per cookie: About 101 calories, 3g protein, 12g carbohydrate, 6g fat, 1g fiber, 0mg cholesterol, 7mg sodium

Peanut Butter Cup Cookies

Submitted by: **Nancy**

"These cookies have a sweet peanut butter cup center."

Prep Time: 15 minutes • **Cook Time:** 8 minutes per batch

1¾ cups all-purpose flour
½ teaspoon salt
1 teaspoon baking soda
½ cup butter, softened
½ cup white sugar
½ cup peanut butter
½ cup packed brown sugar

1 egg, beaten
1 teaspoon vanilla extract
2 tablespoons milk
40 miniature chocolate covered peanut butter cups, unwrapped

1. Preheat oven to 375°F (190°C).

2. Sift together the flour, salt, and baking soda; set aside.

3. Cream together the butter, white sugar, peanut butter, and brown sugar until fluffy. Beat in the egg, vanilla, and milk. Add the flour mixture; mix well.

4. Shape into 40 balls and place each ball into an ungreased mini muffin pan.

5. Bake in the preheated oven for about 8 minutes. Remove from oven and immediately press a mini peanut butter cup into each ball. Cool and carefully remove from pan. **Yield:** 40 cookies.

Per cookie: About 82 calories, 2g protein, 10g carbohydrate, 4g fat, 0g fiber, 12mg cholesterol, 102mg sodium

Melt-In-Your-Mouth Peanut Butter Cookies

Submitted by **Angie M**

"These cookies live up to their name—they melt in your mouth."

Prep Time: 15 minutes • **Cook Time:** 12 minutes per batch

1	cup shortening	2	tablespoons water
1	cup white sugar	2½	cups sifted all–purpose flour
1	cup packed brown sugar	1	teaspoon baking soda
1	cup peanut butter	1	teaspoon salt
2	eggs		

1. Preheat oven to 375°F (190°C).

2. Cream together the shortening, white sugar, brown sugar, and peanut butter until well mixed. Beat in the eggs and the water.

3. Gradually beat in the flour, baking soda, and salt. Form cookies on ungreased baking sheets with a cookie press or roll into balls and flatten with a floured fork or fingers.

4. Bake in the preheated oven for 10 to 12 minutes. Remove from baking sheets and cool on wire racks. **Yield:** 3 dozen.

Per cookie: About 173 calories, 3g protein, 20g carbohydrate, 10g fat, 1g fiber, 12mg cholesterol, 139mg sodium

freezing cookie dough and cookies

Most cookie doughs freeze extremely well and can be kept frozen up to 4 or 6 weeks. Keep in mind that the dough will absorb any odd odors present in your freezer if the dough isn't properly wrapped and sealed. To prevent this smell-sponge effect, wrap the dough securely twice. Write the type of cookie dough and the date it was frozen on the outside of the package. When you're ready to bake, thaw the dough in the refrigerator. This will take several hours, so plan ahead. The cookie doughs that freeze best are shortbreads, chocolate chip, peanut butter, refrigerator, sugar, and brownies. Cakelike cookies, such as madeleines and tuiles, have a very liquidy batter and do not freeze well.

Freezing baked cookies is a great way to preserve their freshness. Baked cookies will keep in the freezer for 3 or 4 weeks. Double-wrap the cookies securely and write the date and the type of cookie on the outside of the package. When you're ready to eat the cookies, let them come to room temperature, or, for you impatient types, pop them in the microwave on high for about 30 seconds.   - Ursula Dalzell, **Allrecipes.com**

Gelatin Spritz Cookies

Submitted by: **Kathy**
"Use your favorite flavor gelatin to make these colorful and easy cookies."

Prep Time: 10 minutes • **Cook Time:** 10 minutes

1½	cups butter, softened	1	teaspoon vanilla extract
1	cup white sugar	3½	cups all-purpose flour
1	(3 ounce) package fruit-flavored gelatin	1	teaspoon baking powder
1	egg	¼	cup white sugar

1. Preheat oven to 400°F (205°C).
2. Cream butter, sugar, and gelatin. Add egg and vanilla. Beat well. Gradually add flour and baking powder. Blend until smooth.
3. Chill dough until firm. Roll dough into balls and press with bottom of glass to flatten. To prevent sticking, dip glass in sugar before pressing. If using a cookie press, do not chill dough before pressing cookies. Place cookies on ungreased baking sheets and bake in the preheated oven for 7 to 10 minutes. Remove from baking sheets and cool on wire racks. **Yield:** 3 dozen.

Per cookie: About 145 calories, 2g protein, 17g carbohydrate, 8g fat, 0g fiber, 27mg cholesterol, 100mg sodium

Molasses Cookies

Submitted by: **Brenda Hall**
"Spicy and chewy, these cookies store well and are great for gift-giving."

Prep Time: 20 minutes • **Cook Time:** 10 minutes per batch

¾	cup butter or margarine, melted	2	teaspoons baking soda
1	cup white sugar	1	teaspoon ground cinnamon
¼	cup molasses	½	teaspoon ground cloves
1	egg	½	teaspoon ground ginger
2	cups all-purpose flour	½	teaspoon salt
		½	cup white sugar

1. Combine the melted butter with the sugar, molasses, and egg.
2. Mix together the flour, baking soda, cinnamon, cloves, ginger, and salt. Gradually add the dry ingredients to the butter mixture and mix until combined. Chill dough for 1 hour.
3. Preheat oven to 375°F (190°C).
4. Shape dough into walnut sized balls and roll them in white sugar. Place balls on a baking sheet and flatten slightly. Bake in the preheated oven for 8 to 10 minutes. Remove from baking sheets and cool on wire racks. **Yield:** 5 dozen.

Per cookie: About 60 calories, 1g protein, 9g carbohydrate, 2g fat, 0g fiber, 4mg cholesterol, 90mg sodium

Chocolate Mice

Submitted by: **Rosina**
"Kids will love these—they're whimsical and fun. To make dark mice, roll the cookies in ⅓ cup finely crushed chocolate wafers instead of the confectioners' sugar."

Prep Time: 20 minutes

4 (1 ounce) squares semisweet chocolate	⅓ cup confectioners' sugar
⅓ cup sour cream	24 silver decorating candy
1 cup finely crushed chocolate wafer cookies	¼ cup sliced almonds
	12 long red string licorice

1. Melt the chocolate and combine with sour cream. Stir in 1 cup crushed chocolate wafer cookies. Mix well. Cover and chill until firm.
2. Roll chocolate mixture by level tablespoonfuls into balls. Mold to a slight point at one end to shape the nose.
3. Roll dough in confectioners' sugar. On each mouse, place 2 silver candies in appropriate spot for eyes, almond slices for ears, and a licorice string for the tail.
4. Refrigerate for at least two hours until firm. **Yield:** 1 dozen.

Per cookie: About 173 calories, 2g protein, 28g carbohydrate, 7g fat, 1g fiber, 3mg cholesterol, 90mg sodium

Cranberry-Pistachio Biscotti

Submitted by: **Gerry Meyer**

"The red and green make a great Christmas cookie. I've used other nuts instead of pistachios with success. If your pistachios are salted, omit the ¼ teaspoon salt from the recipe."

Prep Time: 25 minutes • **Cook Time:** 45 minutes

¼	cup light olive oil	1¾	cups all-purpose flour
¾	cup white sugar	¼	teaspoon salt
2	teaspoons vanilla extract	1	teaspoon baking powder
½	teaspoon almond extract	½	cup dried cranberries
2	eggs	1½	cups pistachios

1. Preheat oven to 300°F (150°C).

2. In a large bowl, mix together oil and sugar until well blended. Mix in the vanilla and almond extracts, then beat in the eggs. Combine flour, salt, and baking powder; gradually stir into egg mixture. Mix in cranberries and nuts by hand.

3. Divide dough in half. Form two 2x12 inch logs on a baking sheet lined with parchment paper. Dough may be sticky; wet hands with cool water to handle dough more easily.

4. Bake in the preheated oven for 35 minutes or until logs are light brown. Remove from oven and set aside to cool for 10 minutes. Reduce heat to 275°F (135°C).

5. Slice logs diagonally into ¾ inch thick slices. Lay on sides on parchment covered baking sheets. Bake approximately 8 to 10 more minutes or until dry. Remove from baking sheets and cool on wire racks. **Yield:** 3 dozen.

Per cookie: About 92 calories, 2g protein, 12g carbohydrate, 4g fat, 1g fiber, 12mg cholesterol, 56mg sodium

Brownie Biscotti

Submitted by: **Linda Foster**

"A chocolate version of an Italian favorite. You can substitute milk for the water in the egg wash, if you wish."

Prep Time: 30 minutes • Cook Time: 40 minutes

⅓ cup butter, softened
⅔ cup white sugar
2 eggs
1 teaspoon vanilla extract
1¾ cups all-purpose flour
⅓ cup unsweetened cocoa powder

2 teaspoons baking powder
½ cup mini semisweet chocolate chips
¼ cup chopped walnuts
1 egg yolk, beaten
1 tablespoon water

1. Preheat oven to 375°F (190°C). Grease baking sheets or line with parchment paper.
2. In a large bowl, cream together the butter and sugar until smooth. Beat in the eggs, one at a time, then stir in the vanilla. Combine the flour, cocoa, and baking powder; stir into the creamed mixture until well blended. Dough will be stiff, so mix in the last bit by hand. Mix in the chocolate chips and walnuts.
3. Divide dough into 2 equal parts. Shape into two 2x9 inch loaves. Place onto baking sheet 4 inches apart. Combine egg yolk and water and brush over loaves.
4. Bake in the preheated oven for 20 to 25 minutes or until firm. Cool on baking sheet for 30 minutes.
5. Using a serrated knife, slice the loaves diagonally into 1 inch slices. Place the slices on ungreased baking sheets, placing slices on their sides. Bake for 10 to 15 more minutes on each side or until dry. Remove from baking sheet and cool on wire racks. **Yield:** 2½ dozen.

Per cookie: About 95 calories, 2g protein, 13g carbohydrate, 4g fat, 1g fiber, 27mg cholesterol, 58mg sodium

Sour Cream Spritz

Submitted by: **Diana Stephens**
"This soft spice spritz cookie has been a holiday tradition for over 20 years."

Prep Time: 20 minutes • Cook Time: 12 minutes per batch

1 cup butter, softened	2¾ cups all-purpose flour
¾ cup white sugar	1 teaspoon ground cinnamon
1 egg yolk	½ teaspoon salt
⅓ cup sour cream	½ teaspoon baking soda
1 teaspoon vanilla extract	

1. Preheat oven to 375°F (190°C).
2. Cream together the butter and sugar. Beat in egg yolk, sour cream, and vanilla. In a separate bowl, mix flour, cinnamon, salt, and baking soda. Stir flour mixture into butter mixture. Place dough into a cookie press and press cookies onto ungreased baking sheets.
3. Bake in the preheated oven 10 to 12 minutes, until golden. Cool 5 minutes on baking sheets before transferring to wire racks to cool completely. **Yield:** 8 dozen.

Per cookie: About 39 calories, 0g protein, 4g carbohydrate, 2g fat, 0g fiber, 8mg cholesterol, 39mg sodium

Norwegian Butter Cookies

Submitted by: **Cookierecipe.com Staff**
"Try using lemon extract in place of the vanilla for a citrusy punch!"

Prep Time: 30 minutes • Cook Time: 12 minutes

2 eggs	1 cup all-purpose flour
½ cup butter, softened	½ teaspoon vanilla extract
¼ cup white sugar	

1. Place whole eggs in a saucepan and cover completely with cold water. Bring water to a boil. Cover, remove from heat, and let eggs stand in hot water for 10 to 12 minutes. Remove from hot water, cool, peel, and separate yolks.

2. Preheat oven to 375°F (190°C).

3. Cream the butter and hard boiled egg yolks. Beat well. Beat in the sugar. Add the flour and vanilla. Mix thoroughly. Put through a cookie press or arrange by teaspoonfuls on an ungreased baking sheet.

4. Bake in the preheated oven for 10 to 12 minutes or until lightly browned. Remove from baking sheet and cool on wire racks. **Yield:** 1 dozen.

Per cookie: About 135 calories, 2g protein, 12g carbohydrate, 9g fat, 0g fiber, 56mg cholesterol, 89mg sodium

Cream Cheese Cookies

Submitted by: **Robin**

"I fill the centers of these pressed cookies with fruit preserves or a chocolate chip for added variety."

Prep Time: 10 minutes • **Cook Time:** 15 minutes per batch

1	cup butter, softened	1	egg yolk
1	(3 ounce) package cream cheese, softened	½	teaspoon vanilla extract
1	cup white sugar	2½	cups all-purpose flour

1. Preheat oven to 325°F (165°C). Lightly grease baking sheets.

2. In a large bowl, cream together butter, cream cheese, and sugar until light and fluffy. Beat in egg yolk and vanilla. Stir in flour until well blended. Drop dough by teaspoonfuls or use a cookie press to place onto prepared baking sheets.

3. Bake in the preheated oven for 15 minutes. Allow cookies to cool slightly on baking sheets before transferring to wire racks to cool completely. **Yield:** 6 dozen.

Per cookie: About 54 calories, 1g protein, 6g carbohydrate, 3g fat, 0g fiber, 11mg cholesterol, 30mg sodium

Langues-de-Chat

Submitted by: **Mary Beth**

"Langues-de-Chat, translated as 'cats' tongues,' are long, thin cookies. These French classics are dipped in melted chocolate for an extra touch."

Prep Time: 15 minutes • **Cook Time:** 10 minutes per batch

½ cup butter, softened	1½ teaspoons vanilla extract
½ cup white sugar	6 (1 ounce) squares
3 egg whites	semisweet chocolate,
1½ cups all-purpose flour	melted

1. Preheat oven to 400°F (205°C). Lightly grease baking sheets. Cream butter and sugar together. Add egg whites, one at a time, mixing well after each addition. Add flour and vanilla. If dough seems too soft, add more flour.

2. Force through a pastry bag or cookie press with a medium star tip onto prepared baking sheets. Make each cookie about 3 inches long.

3. Bake in the preheated oven for 10 minutes or until lightly browned. When cool, dip 1 end of each cookie into melted chocolate and place on wax paper until chocolate hardens. Store in a cool place. **Yield:** 6 dozen.

Per cookie: About 41 calories, 1g protein, 5g carbohydrate, 2g fat, 0g fiber, 4mg cholesterol, 17mg sodium

*P*repare to dip

Decorating with chocolate is easy, but it helps to be organized. First, put chocolate into a heat-proof bowl. Set bowl in a pan of simmering water. A microwave oven also works well for melting chocolate; just be sure to stir every 15 seconds or so.

While the chocolate is melting, arrange your workspace so that the cookies you wish to dip and a couple of cookie sheets lined with parchment or wax paper are side by side. When the chocolate is mostly melted, remove from the heat and continue to stir until smooth and cooled.

Using your hands or tongs, dip cookies halfway into the chocolate and let the excess drip off. Then give the cookie a gentle shake and once again, let the excess drip off. This will keep the chocolate from forming a puddle around the cookie while it sets up. Place the cookies onto the wax paper starting at the farthest end and working inward. This prevents you from dripping onto the finished cookies.   - *Emily Brune,* **Allrecipes.com**

Snow Flakes

Submitted by: **Jessy Davis**
"Use your cookie press for these wonderfully soft and flavorful cookies."

Prep Time: 20 minutes • **Cook Time:** 12 minutes per batch

1	cup butter-flavored shortening	1	teaspoon vanilla extract
1	(3 ounce) package cream cheese, softened	1	teaspoon orange zest
		2½	cups all-purpose flour
1	cup white sugar	½	teaspoon salt
1	egg yolk	¼	teaspoon ground cinnamon

1. Preheat oven to 350°F (175°C).

2. In a medium bowl, cream together shortening, cream cheese, and sugar. Beat in egg yolk, vanilla, and orange zest. Continue creaming until light and fluffy. Gradually stir in flour, salt, and cinnamon. Fill the cookie press and form cookies on ungreased baking sheets.

3. Bake in the preheated oven for 10 to 12 minutes. Remove from baking sheets and cool on wire racks. **Yield:** 6 dozen.

Per cookie: About 59 calories, 1g protein, 6g carbohydrate, 4g fat, 0g fiber, 4mg cholesterol, 20mg sodium

Apple Squares

Submitted by: **BarbiAnn**

"Apples, nuts, and cinnamon make these squares delicious. They last hardly a day at my house!"

Prep Time: 25 minutes • **Cook Time:** 30 minutes

1	cup sifted all-purpose flour	1	egg
1	teaspoon baking powder	1	teaspoon vanilla extract
¼	teaspoon salt	½	cup chopped apple
¼	teaspoon ground cinnamon	½	cup finely chopped walnuts
¼	cup butter, melted	2	teaspoons ground cinnamon
½	cup packed brown sugar		
½	cup white sugar	2	tablespoons white sugar

1. Preheat oven to 350°F (175°C). Grease a 9x9 inch pan. Sift together flour, baking powder, salt, and ¼ teaspoon of cinnamon; set aside.

2. In a large bowl, mix together melted butter, brown sugar, and ½ cup of white sugar until smooth. Stir in the egg and vanilla. Blend in the flour mixture until just combined, then stir in the apple and walnuts. Spread the mixture evenly into the prepared pan. In a small bowl, stir together the remaining cinnamon and sugar; sprinkle over apples and nuts.

3. Bake in the preheated oven for 25 to 30 minutes; top should spring back when lightly touched. Cool in the pan and cut into squares. **Yield:** 16 servings.

Per serving: About 143 calories, 2g protein, 22g carbohydrate, 6g fat, 1g fiber, 21mg cholesterol, 103mg sodium

Bake-Sale Lemon Bars

Submitted by: **Elaine**

"They are very easy to make and fabulously delicious."

Prep Time: 15 minutes • **Cook Time:** 45 minutes

1½ cups all-purpose flour
⅔ cup confectioners' sugar
¾ cup butter, softened
3 eggs
1½ cups white sugar

3 tablespoons all-purpose flour
¼ cup lemon juice
⅓ cup confectioners' sugar

1. Preheat oven to 375°F (190°C). Grease a 9x13 inch baking pan.
2. Combine the flour, ⅔ cup confectioners' sugar, and butter. Pat dough into prepared pan. Bake in the preheated oven for 20 minutes, until slightly golden.
3. While the crust is baking, whisk together eggs, white sugar, flour, and lemon juice until frothy. Pour lemon mixture over the hot crust.
4. Return to the preheated oven for 20 to 25 more minutes or until light golden brown. Cool on a wire rack. Dust the top with confectioners' sugar. Cut into bars. **Yield:** 36 servings.

Per serving: About 107 calories, 1g protein, 16g carbohydrate, 4g fat, 0g fiber, 28mg cholesterol, 45mg sodium

Delicious Raspberry-Oatmeal Cookie Bars

Submitted by: **Holly**
"One of my favorite cookie bar recipes—and so easy to make!"

Prep Time: 15 minutes • **Cook Time:** 40 minutes

½ cup packed light brown sugar	⅛ teaspoon salt
1 cup all-purpose flour	1 cup rolled oats
¼ teaspoon baking soda	½ cup butter, softened
	¾ cup seedless raspberry jam

1. Preheat oven to 350°F (175°C). Grease an 8x8 inch square pan and line with greased foil.
2. Combine brown sugar, flour, baking soda, salt, and rolled oats. Cut in the butter using 2 knives or a pastry blender to form a crumbly mixture. Press 2 cups of the mixture into the prepared pan. Spread the jam to within ¼ inch of the edge. Sprinkle the remaining crumb mixture over top and lightly press it into the jam.
3. Bake in the preheated oven for 35 to 40 minutes or until lightly browned. Allow to cool before cutting into bars. **Yield:** 12 servings.

Per serving: About 244 calories, 3g protein, 39g carbohydrate, 9g fat, 2g fiber, 21mg cholesterol, 143mg sodium

Chewy Granola Bars

Submitted by: **Nancy Burstein**
"Try using any combination of miniature chocolate chips, sunflower seeds, raisins, chopped dried fruits, candy-coated chocolate pieces, or chopped nuts."

Prep Time: 15 minutes • **Cook Time:** 22 minutes

4½ cups rolled oats	½ cup honey
1 cup all-purpose flour	⅓ cup packed brown sugar
1 teaspoon baking soda	2 cups mini semisweet chocolate chips
1 teaspoon vanilla extract	
⅔ cup butter, softened	

1. Preheat oven to 325°F (165°C). Lightly grease one 9x13 inch pan.
2. In a large bowl, combine the oats, flour, baking soda, vanilla, butter, honey, and brown sugar. Stir in the 2 cups chocolate chips.
3. Lightly press mixture into the prepared pan. Bake in the preheated oven for 18 to 22 minutes or until golden brown. Let cool for 10 minutes, then cut into bars. Let bars cool completely in pan before removing or serving. **Yield:** 24 servings.

Per serving: About 295 calories, 6g protein, 43g carbohydrate, 12g fat, 3g fiber, 14mg cholesterol, 107mg sodium

Chocolate-Peanut Butter Bars IV

Submitted by: **Justine**
"These bars are a classic blend of peanut butter and chocolate."

Prep Time: 15 minutes

2½   cups graham cracker
    crumbs
2¾   cups confectioners' sugar
 1   cup peanut butter

1   cup butter, melted
2   cups semisweet chocolate
  chips

1. In a medium bowl, stir together graham cracker crumbs, confectioners' sugar, peanut butter, and melted butter. Press firmly into a 9x13 inch pan.
2. Melt chocolate chips over a double boiler or in the microwave on high for 2 minutes or until melted, stirring occasionally. Spread melted chocolate over the crumb crust. Chill for about 5 minutes, then cut into bars before the chocolate is completely set. Chill until ready to serve. **Yield:** 24 servings.

Per serving: About 289 calories, 4g protein, 31g carbohydrate, 18g fat, 2g fiber, 21mg cholesterol, 183mg sodium

Baseball Bars

Submitted by: **L. Callero**

"These bars are very rich and sweet. They make a wonderful treat."

Prep Time: 20 minutes • **Cook Time:** 15 minutes

⅔ cup butter
1 cup packed brown sugar
¼ cup light corn syrup
¼ cup crunchy peanut butter
1 teaspoon vanilla extract
4 cups quick cooking oats

2 cups semisweet chocolate chips
2 cups butterscotch chips
⅔ cup crunchy peanut butter
1 cup chopped unsalted peanuts (optional)

1. Preheat oven to 375°F (190°C). Grease one 9x13 inch pan.

2. In a saucepan over medium heat, melt the butter, brown sugar, and corn syrup together. Stir in ¼ cup peanut butter and the vanilla. Mix well and stir in the oats. Press the mixture into the prepared pan.

3. Bake in the preheated oven for 15 minutes.

4. In the top of a double boiler, melt the chocolate chips and butterscotch chips together. Stir in ⅔ cup peanut butter and the chopped nuts, if desired. Stir until well blended.

5. Spread the topping over the warm cooked bars. Sprinkle with additional chopped nuts, if desired. Cool on a wire rack and refrigerate. Cut into bars once chilled. **Yield:** 20 servings.

Per serving: About 524 calories, 10g protein, 61g carbohydrate, 28g fat, 5g fiber, 17mg cholesterol, 150mg sodium

Caramel Shortbread Squares

Submitted by: **Julia**

"These cookies consist of a shortbread crust, firm caramel center, and a milk chocolate top."

Prep Time: 30 minutes • **Cook Time:** 50 minutes

⅔ cup butter, softened
¼ cup white sugar
1¼ cups all-purpose flour
½ cup butter
½ cup packed light brown sugar

2 tablespoons light corn syrup
½ cup sweetened condensed milk
1¼ cups milk chocolate chips

1. Preheat oven to 350°F (175°C). Grease a 9x9 inch square pan.
2. In a medium bowl, mix together ⅔ cup butter, white sugar, and flour until evenly crumbly. Press into prepared pan. Bake in the pre-heated oven for 20 minutes.
3. In a 2 quart heavy saucepan, combine ½ cup butter, brown sugar, corn syrup, and sweetened condensed milk. Bring to a boil over medium-high heat, about 8 minutes. Reduce heat to medium and continue to boil 22 minutes or until caramel-colored. Remove from heat and beat vigorously with a wooden spoon for about 3 minutes. Pour over baked crust. Cool until it begins to firm, about 20 to 25 minutes.
4. Melt chocolate chips and pour over caramel layer. Cover the layer completely. Chill. Cut into squares. **Yield:** 16 servings.

Per serving: About 297 calories, 2g protein, 33g carbohydrate, 19g fat, 0g fiber, 42mg cholesterol, 155mg sodium

Candy Bar Brownies

Submitted by: **Madonna**

"Brownies made with candy bars are the perfect after-school snack. Use your favorite candy bar."

Prep Time: 15 minutes • **Cook Time:** 30 minutes

1 (18.25 ounce) package German chocolate cake mix

¾ cup melted butter

⅔ cup sweetened condensed milk

4 (2.16 ounce) chocolate-coated caramel peanut nougat bars, chopped

1. Preheat oven to 350°F (175°C). Grease a 9x13 inch pan. Mix cake mix with melted butter and condensed milk. Spread half of the mixture into prepared pan.

2. Bake in the preheated oven for 10 minutes.

3. Layer chopped candy bars on top of the baked crust. Crumble remaining batter on top of the candy bars.

4. Return to the oven and bake 20 more minutes. Let cool in pan and cut into bars. **Yield:** 24 servings.

Per serving: About 216 calories, 3g protein, 27g carbohydrate, 11g fat, 1g fiber, 20mg cholesterol, 230mg sodium

ining lesson

When baking brownies, lining the pan with foil can make your life a little easier. Lightly grease the pan and line with foil before spreading the batter in the pan. Lift the foil with uncut baked brownies out of the pan. Remove the foil, and the brownies will be easy to cut and remove. No more wasting the first cut brownie!

Blonde Brownies

Submitted by: **Sue Bush**
"Rich, chewy brownies crowned with chocolate chips are irresistible."

Prep Time: 20 minutes • **Cook Time:** 25 minutes

1	cup sifted all-purpose flour	1	cup packed brown sugar
½	teaspoon baking powder	1	egg, lightly beaten
⅛	teaspoon baking soda	1	tablespoon vanilla extract
½	teaspoon salt	1	cup semisweet chocolate
½	cup chopped walnuts		chips
⅓	cup butter		

1. Preheat oven to 350°F (175°C). Grease a 9x9 inch square pan.
2. Combine sifted flour, baking powder, baking soda, and salt. Sift again and add ½ cup chopped nuts. Mix well and set aside.
3. Melt ⅓ cup butter. Add 1 cup firmly packed brown sugar and mix well. Cool slightly.
4. Add beaten egg and vanilla; blend well. Add flour mixture, a little at a time, mixing well.
5. Spread into prepared pan. Sprinkle chocolate chips on top. Bake in the preheated oven for 20 to 25 minutes. Cool and cut into bars.
Yield: 1 dozen.

Per serving: About 239 calories, 3g protein, 33g carbohydrate, 12g fat, 1g fiber, 32mg cholesterol, 196mg sodium

Index